The Big Day!
First Day at School

Nicola Barber

First published in 2008 by Wayland

This paperback edition published in 2011 by Wayland

Copyright © Wayland 2008

Wayland
338 Euston Road
London NW1 3BH

Wayland Australia
Level 17/207 Kent Street
Sydney, NSW 2000

Editor: Camilla Lloyd
Designer: Elaine Wilkinson
Picture Researcher: Kathy Lockley

Picture Acknowledgments: The author and publisher would like to thank the following for their pictures to be reproduced in this publication: Cover photograph and 20: Adrian Sherratt/Alamy Images; Angela Hampton/Bubbles Photolibrary:10; Chris Fairclough: 14, 15; Gideon mendel/Corbis: 13, 19; Janine Wiedel Photo Library/Alamy Images: 5; Jennie Hart/Alamy Images: 21; Jennie Woodcock/Bubbles Photolibrary: 7; Matt Henry Gunther/Taxi/Getty Images: 9; Olaf Doering/Alamy Images: 6; Ronnie Kaufman/Corbis: 12, 24; Sally & Richard Greenhill/Alamy Images: 1, 18; Steve Skjold/Alamy Images: 11; Teegan Mason: 17; Wayland Archive: 16; www.shoutpictures.com: 8.

British Library Cataloguing in Publication Data:
Barber, Nicola
  First day at school. - (The big day)
  1.First day of school - Juvenile literature
  I. Title
  372

ISBN: 978 0 7502 6516 4

Printed in China

Wayland is a division of Hachette Children's Books, an Hachette UK company

Contents

Starting school

Soon it will be the big day – your first day at school.

What will school be like?

You have probably visited your new school, and met your new teacher. Have you talked to your brother or sister about school?

Your Mum or Dad might read you some stories
about going to school.

Getting ready

What will you wear at your new school?
In some schools children wear their normal,
everyday clothes.

In other schools children wear special clothes,
called a uniform. Your Mum or Dad will take
you to buy the clothes you need for school.

You will need a book bag to carry your books and work. You might need to choose a lunchbox too.

Going to school

How will you get to school?
If you live close by you might be able
to walk, or go on your bike.

If you live further away, your Mum or Dad may take you in the car. Or you might go by bus, or train.

Saying goodbye

When you get to school your
teacher will be there to
say hello.

You say goodbye
to your parents.
You might feel
a bit sad, but
you will see
them again in
the afternoon.

You can hang your coat and bag on a peg in the cloakroom. Your teacher will show you where your classroom is.

In your classroom

There are all sort of things
to do in your classroom.
You can draw or paint,
or make models.
You can play with
sand or water.

You can look at books, or practise writing.
Sometimes you might go to a different room
to work on the school computers.

Playtime

Playtime is fun!
If the weather is nice you can go outside.

Some schools have equipment for climbing, swinging and sliding. You can play games in the playground too.

If you are feeling a bit lonely or sad
you can sit on the friendship bench and
someone will look after you.

Lunchtime

It's lunchtime and you are hungry. Your teacher will take you to the school dining room, or to the hall that is used for lunch.

The lunchtime assistants will help you to choose your lunch. There's pudding too!

You might pack your own lunch at home
in a lunchbox and bring that to school.

Making friends

You might already know some of the children in your class. You will soon start to make new friends too.

At playtime you can play games with
your friends.

Going home

When it is time to go home, everyone helps to tidy up the classroom. Then your teacher might read a story, or you might sing some songs.

You collect your bag and coat from your peg. Your teacher says goodbye and makes sure there is someone to meet you and to take you home safely.

How was your first day?

School words

If you are writing about starting school, these are some of the words you might need to use.

Classroom

Lunchbox

Cloakroom

Peg

Equipment

Playtime

Friendship bench

Story

Hometime

Teacher

Lunch

Uniform

Further information

Books

Billy and the Big New School by Laurence Anholt, Orchard Books, 2004

Do I Have to Go to School?: A First Look at Starting School by Lesley Harker, Hodder Children's Books, 2006

Going to School (Usborne First Experiences) by Anne Civardi, Usborne Publishing, 2002

I Am Too Absolutely Small for School by Lauren Child, Orchard Books, 2004

Starting School, Parragon Publishing, 2006

Topsy and Tim Start School by Jean and Gareth Adamson, Ladybird Books, 2003

Websites for parents

http://www.savethechildren.org.uk/scuk/jsp/resources/details.jsp?id=1769

http://www.bbc.co.uk/parenting/your_kids/primary_starting.shtml

http://www.raisingkids.co.uk/1_4/tod_care08.asp

http://www.direct.gov.uk/en/EducationAndLearning/PreschoolLearning/PreparingForthe FirstDayAtSchool/index.htm

http://www.parentscentre.gov.uk/foragegroup/3to5years/beforeyourchildstartsschool/

Index